RAIMAZ Publishing
2019

First RAIMAZ Printing, June 2019
10 9 8 7 6 5 4 3 2 1

RAIMAZPublishing.com

ISBN 978-0-359-71945-7

RESEARCH**MASTER**

RESEARCH**MASTER** is designed to help you maximize your research. Each one of these journals is small, lightweight and has the right forms to help you with your research. Focusing on three main areas
1- Tasks Items (You can keep track of your efforts)
2- Memory Joggers (Sites you've visted / username and passwords / other vital reminders)
3 - Notes, and REFINED notes. (You'll take notes on left side of booklet and then refine them on the right side. Or use this however you wish!)

Owner:_____

Phone: _____ EMAIL:_____

If found, please return to the owner listed above!

Included in each one of the RESEARCH**MASTER** Journals is:
MEMORY**JOGGER** (5 Sheets - 42 items a sheet)
Task**KILLER** Items (5 Sheets - Track 43 tasks a sheet)
Research Notes (18 Spreads... Notes on left, details on right)

More than enough space to research mutliple projects and track the details that are vital to the success of your efforts.

MEMORY**JOGGER**

MEMORY ITEM OF IMPORTANCE: (example - meeting note, server name, serial number, order date, etc.) **NOTE:** (example - could be password, code, hint, etc.)

MEMORY**JOGGER**

MEMORY ITEM OF **IMPORTANCE:** (example - meeting note, server name, serial number, order date, etc.)   **NOTE:** (example - could be password, code, hint, etc.)

MEMORY**JOGGER**

MEMORY ITEM OF **IMPORTANCE**: (example - meeting note, server name, serial number, order date, etc.)	**NOTE**: (example - could be password, code, hint, etc.)

MEMORY**JOGGER**

MEMORY ITEM OF **IMPORTANCE:** (example - meeting note, server name, serial number, order date, etc.)   **NOTE:** (example - could be password, code, hint, etc.)

MEMORY**JOGGER**

MEMORY ITEM OF **IMPORTANCE:** (example - meeting note, server name, serial number, order date, etc.)	**NOTE:** (example - could be password, code, hint, etc.)

MEMORY**JOGGER**

MEMORY ITEM OF **IMPORTANCE**: (example - meeting note, server name, serial number, order date, etc.)   **NOTE**: (example - could be password, code, hint, etc.)

ASK:	DUE DATE:	XP:	5%	20%	40%	60%	80%	DONE!

TOTAL XP:

SPECIAL NOTES:

TASK:	DUE DATE:	XP:	5%	20%	40%	60%	80%	DON

SPECIAL NOTES:

TOTAL XP:

TASK:	DUE DATE:	XP:	5%	20%	40%	60%	80%	DONE!

TOTAL XP:

SPECIAL NOTES:

TASK:	DUE DATE:	XP:	5%	20%	40%	60%	80%	DON
			☐	☐	☐	☐	☐	☐
			☐	☐	☐	☐	☐	☐
			☐	☐	☐	☐	☐	☐
			☐	☐	☐	☐	☐	☐
			☐	☐	☐	☐	☐	☐
			☐	☐	☐	☐	☐	☐
			☐	☐	☐	☐	☐	☐
			☐	☐	☐	☐	☐	☐
			☐	☐	☐	☐	☐	☐
			☐	☐	☐	☐	☐	☐
			☐	☐	☐	☐	☐	☐
			☐	☐	☐	☐	☐	☐
			☐	☐	☐	☐	☐	☐
			☐	☐	☐	☐	☐	☐
			☐	☐	☐	☐	☐	☐
			☐	☐	☐	☐	☐	☐
			☐	☐	☐	☐	☐	☐
			☐	☐	☐	☐	☐	☐
			☐	☐	☐	☐	☐	☐
			☐	☐	☐	☐	☐	☐
			☐	☐	☐	☐	☐	☐
			☐	☐	☐	☐	☐	☐
			☐	☐	☐	☐	☐	☐
			☐	☐	☐	☐	☐	☐
			☐	☐	☐	☐	☐	☐
			☐	☐	☐	☐	☐	☐
			☐	☐	☐	☐	☐	☐
			☐	☐	☐	☐	☐	☐
			☐	☐	☐	☐	☐	☐
			☐	☐	☐	☐	☐	☐
			☐	☐	☐	☐	☐	☐
			☐	☐	☐	☐	☐	☐
			☐	☐	☐	☐	☐	☐
			☐	☐	☐	☐	☐	☐
			☐	☐	☐	☐	☐	☐
			☐	☐	☐	☐	☐	☐
			☐	☐	☐	☐	☐	☐
			☐	☐	☐	☐	☐	☐
			☐	☐	☐	☐	☐	☐
			☐	☐	☐	☐	☐	☐
			☐	☐	☐	☐	☐	☐
			☐	☐	☐	☐	☐	☐
			☐	☐	☐	☐	☐	☐

SPECIAL NOTES:　　　　　　　　**TOTAL XP:** ☐

ASK: | **DUE DATE:** | **XP:** | **5%** | **20%** | **40%** | **60%** | **80%** | **DONE!**

TASK:	DUE DATE:	XP:	5%	20%	40%	60%	80%	DONE!

TOTAL XP:

PECIAL NOTES:

DATE: _____ SUBJECT: _____ SPECIAL: _____

PRIMARY TOPIC : _____

VITAL BITS #1 (The most important bit of information from today's notes goes here)

VITAL BITS #2 (Continuation of #1 or additional information to be EXTRA prepared!)

VITAL BITS #3 (Continuation of #1 or maximum effort to be RESEARCHMASTER!!!!!! ;) You over-achiever!)

IF YOU ALSO TOOK NOTES ON LAPTOP OR OTHER DEVICE WHAT WAS NAME AND PATH OF FILE?: _____

DATE: _____ SUBJECT: _____ SPECIAL: _____

PRIMARY TOPIC : _____

VITAL BITS #1 (The most important bit of information from today's notes goes here)

VITAL BITS #2 (Continuation of #1 or additional information to be EXTRA prepared!)

VITAL BITS #3 (Continuation of #1 or maximum effort to be RESEARCHMASTER!!!!!! ;) You over-achiever!)

IF YOU ALSO TOOK NOTES ON LAPTOP OR OTHER DEVICE WHAT WAS NAME AND PATH OF FILE?: _____

DATE: _____ SUBJECT: _____ SPECIAL: _____

PRIMARY TOPIC: _____

VITAL BITS #1 (The most important bit of information from today's notes goes here)

VITAL BITS #2 (Continuation of #1 or additional information to be EXTRA prepared!)

VITAL BITS #3 (Continuation of #1 or maximum effort to be RESEARCHMASTER!!!!!! ;) You over-achiever!)

IF YOU ALSO TOOK NOTES ON LAPTOP OR OTHER DEVICE WHAT WAS NAME AND PATH OF FILE?: _____

DATE: _____ SUBJECT: _____ SPECIAL: _____

PRIMARY TOPIC : _____

VITAL BITS #1 (The most important bit of information from today's notes goes here)

VITAL BITS #2 (Continuation of #1 or additional information to be EXTRA prepared!)

VITAL BITS #3 (Continuation of #1 or maximum effort to be RESEARCHMASTER!!!!!! ;) You over-achiever!)

IF YOU ALSO TOOK NOTES ON LAPTOP OR OTHER DEVICE WHAT WAS NAME AND PATH OF FILE?: _____

DATE: _____ SUBJECT: _____ SPECIAL: _____

PRIMARY TOPIC : _____

VITAL BITS #1 (The most important bit of information from today's notes goes here)

VITAL BITS #2 (Continuation of #1 or additional information to be EXTRA prepared!)

VITAL BITS #3 (Continuation of #1 or maximum effort to be RESEARCHMASTER!!!!!! ;) You over-achiever!)

IF YOU ALSO TOOK NOTES ON LAPTOP OR OTHER DEVICE WHAT WAS NAME AND PATH OF FILE?: _____

DATE: _____ SUBJECT: _____ SPECIAL: _____

PRIMARY TOPIC : _____

VITAL BITS #1 (The most important bit of information from today's notes goes here)

VITAL BITS #2 (Continuation of #1 or additional information to be EXTRA prepared!)

VITAL BITS #3 (Continuation of #1 or maximum effort to be RESEARCHMASTER!!!!!! ;) You over-achiever!)

IF YOU ALSO TOOK NOTES ON LAPTOP OR OTHER DEVICE WHAT WAS NAME AND PATH OF FILE?: _____

DATE: SUBJECT: SPECIAL:

PRIMARY TOPIC:

VITAL BITS #1 (The most important bit of information from today's notes goes here)

VITAL BITS #2 (Continuation of #1 or additional information to be EXTRA prepared!)

VITAL BITS #3 (Continuation of #1 or maximum effort to be RESEARCHMASTER!!!!!! ;) You over-achiever!)

IF YOU ALSO TOOK NOTES ON LAPTOP OR OTHER DEVICE WHAT WAS NAME AND PATH OF FILE?:

DATE:_____ SUBJECT:_____ SPECIAL:_____

PRIMARY TOPIC :_____

VITAL BITS #1 (The most important bit of information from today's notes goes here)

VITAL BITS #2 (Continuation of #1 or additional information to be EXTRA prepared!)

VITAL BITS #3 (Continuation of #1 or maximum effort to be RESEARCHMASTER!!!!!! ;) You over-achiever!)

IF YOU ALSO TOOK NOTES ON LAPTOP OR OTHER DEVICE WHAT WAS NAME AND PATH OF FILE?:_____

DATE: SUBJECT: SPECIAL:

PRIMARY TOPIC :

VITAL BITS #1 (The most important bit of information from today's notes goes here)

VITAL BITS #2 (Continuation of #1 or additional information to be EXTRA prepared!)

VITAL BITS #3 (Continuation of #1 or maximum effort to be RESEARCHMASTER!!!!!! ;) You over-achiever!)

IF YOU ALSO TOOK NOTES ON LAPTOP OR OTHER DEVICE WHAT WAS NAME AND PATH OF FILE?:

DATE: _____ SUBJECT: _____ SPECIAL: _____

PRIMARY TOPIC: _____

VITAL BITS #1 (The most important bit of information from today's notes goes here)

VITAL BITS #2 (Continuation of #1 or additional information to be EXTRA prepared!)

VITAL BITS #3 (Continuation of #1 or maximum effort to be RESEARCHMASTER!!!!!! ;) You over-achiever!)

IF YOU ALSO TOOK NOTES ON LAPTOP OR OTHER DEVICE WHAT WAS NAME AND PATH OF FILE?: _____

DATE: SUBJECT: SPECIAL:

PRIMARY TOPIC :

VITAL BITS #1 (The most important bit of information from today's notes goes here)

VITAL BITS #2 (Continuation of #1 or additional information to be EXTRA prepared!)

VITAL BITS #3 (Continuation of #1 or maximum effort to be RESEARCHMASTER!!!!!! ;) You over-achiever!)

IF YOU ALSO TOOK NOTES ON LAPTOP OR OTHER DEVICE WHAT WAS NAME AND PATH OF FILE?:

DATE: SUBJECT: SPECIAL:

PRIMARY TOPIC:

VITAL BITS #1 (The most important bit of information from today's notes goes here)

VITAL BITS #2 (Continuation of #1 or additional information to be EXTRA prepared!)

VITAL BITS #3 (Continuation of #1 or maximum effort to be RESEARCHMASTER!!!!!! ;) You over-achiever!)

IF YOU ALSO TOOK NOTES ON LAPTOP OR OTHER DEVICE WHAT WAS NAME AND PATH OF FILE?:

DATE: _____ SUBJECT: _____ SPECIAL: _____

PRIMARY TOPIC : _____

VITAL BITS #1 (The most important bit of information from today's notes goes here)

VITAL BITS #2 (Continuation of #1 or additional information to be EXTRA prepared!)

VITAL BITS #3 (Continuation of #1 or maximum effort to be RESEARCHMASTER!!!!!! ;) You over-achiever!)

IF YOU ALSO TOOK NOTES ON LAPTOP OR OTHER DEVICE WHAT WAS NAME AND PATH OF FILE?: _____

DATE: _____ SUBJECT: _____ SPECIAL: _____

PRIMARY TOPIC: _____

VITAL BITS #1 (The most important bit of information from today's notes goes here)

VITAL BITS #2 (Continuation of #1 or additional information to be EXTRA prepared!)

VITAL BITS #3 (Continuation of #1 or maximum effort to be RESEARCHMASTER!!!!!! ;) You over-achiever!)

IF YOU ALSO TOOK NOTES ON LAPTOP OR OTHER DEVICE WHAT WAS NAME AND PATH OF FILE?: _____

DATE: _____ SUBJECT: _____ SPECIAL: _____

PRIMARY TOPIC : _____

VITAL BITS #1 (The most important bit of information from today's notes goes here)

VITAL BITS #2 (Continuation of #1 or additional information to be EXTRA prepared!)

VITAL BITS #3 (Continuation of #1 or maximum effort to be RESEARCHMASTER!!!!!! ;) You over-achiever!)

IF YOU ALSO TOOK NOTES ON LAPTOP OR OTHER DEVICE WHAT WAS NAME AND PATH OF FILE?: _____

DATE: _____ SUBJECT: _____ SPECIAL: _____

PRIMARY TOPIC: _____

VITAL BITS #1 (The most important bit of information from today's notes goes here)

VITAL BITS #2 (Continuation of #1 or additional information to be EXTRA prepared!)

VITAL BITS #3 (Continuation of #1 or maximum effort to be RESEARCHMASTER!!!!!! ;) You over-achiever!)

IF YOU ALSO TOOK NOTES ON LAPTOP OR OTHER DEVICE WHAT WAS NAME AND PATH OF FILE?: _____

DATE: _____ SUBJECT: _____ SPECIAL: _____

PRIMARY TOPIC: _____

VITAL BITS #1 (The most important bit of information from today's notes goes here)

VITAL BITS #2 (Continuation of #1 or additional information to be EXTRA prepared!)

VITAL BITS #3 (Continuation of #1 or maximum effort to be RESEARCHMASTER!!!!!! ;) You over-achiever!)

IF YOU ALSO TOOK NOTES ON LAPTOP OR OTHER DEVICE WHAT WAS NAME AND PATH OF FILE?: _____

DATE: _____ SUBJECT: _____ SPECIAL: _____

PRIMARY TOPIC : _____

VITAL BITS #1 (The most important bit of information from today's notes goes here)

VITAL BITS #2 (Continuation of #1 or additional information to be EXTRA prepared!)

VITAL BITS #3 (Continuation of #1 or maximum effort to be RESEARCHMASTER!!!!!! ;) You over-achiever!)

IF YOU ALSO TOOK NOTES ON LAPTOP OR OTHER DEVICE WHAT WAS NAME AND PATH OF FILE?: _____

More amazing Journals can be found at:

http://www.RAIMAZPUBLISHING.com